THE

GW01003753

(

*With explanatory notes
and review questions*
by

Roderick Lawson

CHRISTIAN
HERITAGE

This edition © Christian Focus Publications, 2017
Hardback ISBN: 978-1-78191-810-4
Paperback ISBN: 978-1-85792-288-2

First published in 1997,
reprinted 2002, 2003, 2005, 2007, 2008 and 2011
in the
Christian Heritage Imprint
by
Christian Focus Publications
Geanies House, Fearn, Ross-shire,
IV20 1TW, Great Britain.
www.christianfocus.com

Cover design by Daniel van Straaten

Printed & bound in China

CONTENTS

THE APOSTLES' CREED

I believe in God the Father Almighty, Maker of heaven and earth, and in Jesus Christ his only Son our Lord, who was conceived by the Holy Ghost, born of the Virgin Mary, suffered under Pontius Pilate, was crucified, dead, and buried; he descended into hell★; the third day he rose again from the dead; he ascended into heaven, and sitteth on the right hand of God the Father Almighty; from hence he shall come to judge the quick and the dead. I believe in the Holy Ghost; the holy catholic church; the communion of saints; the forgiveness of sins; the resurrection of the body; and the life everlasting. Amen.

★ *Continued in the state of the dead, and under the power of death, till the third day.*

PREFACE

A catechism is a book in which instruction is conveyed by means of question and answer. This catechism is called the *Shorter Catechism* to distinguish it from another written by the same persons, called the *Larger Catechism*. It was written about the year 1647, by a number of ministers and others who assembled at Westminster, London, to make preparations for a common church and faith for the whole kingdom. It consists of 107 questions and answers. Of these, the first three are introductory. The next thirty-three (4-39) tell us *what to believe*. The next sixty-nine (39-107) tells us *what we are to do*.

Although ostensibly intended only for those 'who are of weaker capacity', the *Shorter Catechism* has always been found in practice to be a hard book to beginners. Hence the necessity for helps and explanations. In this edition, the questions are divided into short sections. The emphatic words and clauses in each answer are marked, in order that the sense may be gathered more readily. The meaning of each answer is given in a short commentary, to provide the pupil with materials for answering the questions of the teacher. Scripture proofs are given in full. At the end of the book, there are revising questions for each catechism question.

INTRODUCTORY

1. **What is the chief end of man?**
A. Man's chief end is to glorify God, and to enjoy him for ever.

Comment

The chief end of a thing means the chief purpose for which it is made. For instance, the chief end of a window is to let in light. Man's chief end is to serve God; and if he do so faithfully on earth, he will be happy with him for ever in heaven.

Proofs

Whether therefore ye eat, or drink, or whatsoever ye do, do all to the glory of God (1 Cor. 10:31).

Therefore are they before the throne of God, and serve him day and night in his temple: and he that sitteth on the throne shall dwell among them. They shall hunger no more, neither thirst any more; neither shall the sun light on them, nor any heat. For the Lamb which is in the midst of the throne shall feed them, and shall lead them unto living fountains of waters: and God shall wipe away all tears from their eyes. (Rev. 7:15-17).

2.   **What rule hath God given to direct us how we may glorify and enjoy him?**

A.   The Word of God, which is contained in the Scriptures of the Old and New Testaments, is the *only* rule to direct us how we may glorify and enjoy him.

Comment

The last answer tells us *the end for which we are made*; this tells us *where to find directions for attaining that end*. We could not know of ourselves how to serve God. But God has told us. He has told us in the Bible. To it, therefore, we must go in order to learn the way of duty.

Proofs

All scripture is given by inspiration of God, and is profitable for doctrine, for reproof, for correction, for instruction in righteousness (2 Tim. 3:16).

And are built upon the foundation of the apostles and prophets, Jesus Christ himself being the chief corner stone (Eph. 2:20).

3.   **What do the Scriptures principally teach?**

A.   The Scriptures principally teach what man is to believe concerning God, and what duty God requires of man.

Comment

In order to attain the chief end of our life, the two things most important for us to know are: What we are to believe, and What we are to do. These two things the Bible explains to us very fully. It tells us what God is, and has done for us, and also what he requires us to do, in order that it may be well with us now and hereafter.

Proofs

Search the scriptures; for in them ye think ye have eternal life: and they are they which testify of me (John 5:39).

Let us hear the conclusion of the whole matter: Fear God, and keep his commandments: for this is the whole duty of man (Eccles. 12:13).

DIVISION 1:
WHAT WE ARE TO BELIEVE

1. WHAT GOD IS

4. **What is God?**

A. God is a spirit – *infinite, eternal*, and *unchangeable* – in his being, wisdom, power, holiness, justice, goodness, and truth.

Comment

The first thing we are here told concerning God is, that he has no *body* as we have. The second thing is, that he is not limited like us by want of power, affected by time, or subject to change. And the third thing is, that in character he is wise, and holy, and just, and good, and true. This is *our* God – the greatest of all beings, and the best.

Proofs

God is a Spirit (John 4:24).

Canst thou by searching find out God? Canst thou find out the Almighty unto perfection? (Job 11:7).

He doeth according to his will in the army of heaven, and among the inhabitants of the earth:

and none can stay his hand, or say unto him, What doest thou? (Dan. 4:35).

Before the mountains were brought forth, or ever thou hadst formed the earth and the world, even from everlasting to everlasting, thou art God (Ps. 90:2).

They shall perish, but thou shalt endure: yea, all of them shall wax old like a garment; as a vesture shalt thou change them, and they shall be changed: but thou art the same, and thy years shall have no end (Ps. 102:26-27).

5.   Are there more Gods than one?

A.   There is but *one* only, the living and true God.

Comment

We are here taught that there is only one God; and this one God is the source of all life, and the only true object of worship.

Proof

I am the LORD, and there is none else, there is no God beside me (Isa. 45:5).

6.   **How many persons are there in the Godhead?**

A.   There are *three* persons in the Godhead – the Father, the Son, and the Holy Ghost; and these three are *one* God, the same in substance, equal in power and glory.

Comment

The Bible tells us that the Father is God, the Son is God, and the Holy Spirit is God. And yet it tells us that these three persons form only *one* God, exist and act together as one, and must be honoured and worshipped alike. This is a subject on which we know nothing except what is revealed.

Proofs

Go ye therefore, and teach all nations, baptizing them in the name of the Father, and of the Son, and of the Holy Ghost (Matt. 28:19).

Hear, O Israel: the LORD our God is one LORD (Deut. 6:4).

2. WHAT GOD HAS DONE

7.   **What are the decrees of God?**

A.   The decrees of God are his eternal purpose, according to the counsel of his will, whereby, for his own glory, he hath *fore-ordained* whatsoever comes to pass.

Comment

The decrees of God are *his purposes*, or *what he has from eternity determined to do*. And this answer tells us that God has so appointed everything that comes to pass. Nothing happens by chance. Everything is arranged upon a plan, and that plan is the plan of God. He makes all things work together for good to them that love him, and for evil to them that hate him.

Proofs

Who hath directed the Spirit of the LORD, or being his counsellor hath taught him? With whom took he counsel, and who instructed him, and taught him in the path of judgment, and taught him knowledge, and shewed to him the way of understanding? (Isa. 40:13-14).

And we know that all things work together for good to them that love God, to them who are the called according to his purpose (Rom. 8:28).

Are not two sparrows sold for a farthing? And one
of them shall not fall on the ground without your
Father (Matt. 10:29).

8.   How doth God execute his decrees?

A.   God executeth his decrees in the works of
creation and providence.

Comment

We have been told what God *is*; we now begin to
learn what he *has done*. We are here told that he
created all things, and still sustains them, and that
in creation and providence we see God executing
his own decrees.

Proofs

Thou art worthy, O Lord, to receive glory and
honour and power: for thou hast created all things,
and for thy pleasure they are and were created
(Rev. 4:11).

He doeth according to his will in the army of
heaven, and among the inhabitants of the earth:
and none can stay his hand, or say unto him, What
doest thou? (Dan. 4:35).

3. CREATION

9. What is the work of creation?

A   The work of creation is God's making all
     things of nothing, by the *word* of his power,
     in the space of *six days*, and all *very good*.

Comment

The first thing that God did in relation to us was to
make the world we live in. Now, when we wish to
make anything, we require materials. Thus, to make
a chair, we need wood. But God made all things *of
nothing*, by merely speaking the word. We are here
told also of the time in which he made all things – six
days; and of the condition in which they were when
made – very good.

Proofs

  Through faith we understand that the worlds were
  framed by the word of God, so that things which
  are seen were not made of things which do appear
  (Heb. 11:3).

  And God saw everything that he had made, and,
  behold, it was very good (Gen. 1:31).

10. How did God create man?

A. God created man, male and female, after his own image, in knowledge, righteousness, and holiness, with dominion over the creatures.

Comment

We are here told that man was created in the likeness of God. His soul resembles God in being upright and holy, and possessed of reason. None of the other animals were so endowed, and they accordingly were put in subjection to him.

Proofs

So God created man in his own image, in the image of God created he him; male and female created he them (Gen. 1:27).

And that ye put on the new man, which after God is created in righteousness and true holiness (Eph. 4:24).

And God blessed them, and God said unto them: Be fruitful, and multiply, and replenish the earth, and subdue it: and have dominion over the fish of the sea, and over the fowl of the air, and over every living thing that moveth upon the earth (Gen. 1:28).

4. PROVIDENCE

11.   What are God's works of providence?

A.   God's works of providence are, his most holy, wise, and powerful preserving and governing all his creatures and all their actions.

Comment

The power of God is quite as necessary to maintain the world as to make it. We cannot live of ourselves. It is *in God* that all things live, and move, and have their being. And so this answer informs us that God not only created everything, but that he cares for his own glory.

Proofs

Behold the fowls of the air: for they sow not, neither do they reap, nor gather into barns; yet your heavenly Father feedeth them (Matt. 6:26).

A man's heart deviseth his way: but the LORD directeth his steps (Prov. 16:9).

His kingdom ruleth over all (Ps. 103:19).

12. **What special act of providence did God exercise toward man in the estate wherein he was created?**

A. When God had created man, he entered into a covenant of life with him, upon condition of *perfect obedience*, forbidding him to eat of the tree of the knowledge of good and evil, upon the pain of *death*.

Comment

When God made Adam and Eve, he said that if they kept his commands, they should live for ever; but if they broke his commands, they should die. This was the *Covenant of Life*. God then put forth his first command, which was that they should not eat of a particular tree, called the tree of the knowledge of good and evil. Their regard for this would show how far they were willing to obey him in all things.

Proofs

And the LORD God commanded the man, saying: Of every tree of the garden thou mayest freely eat; but of the tree of the knowledge of good and evil, thou shalt not eat of it: for in the day that thou eatest thereof thou shalt surely die (Gen. 2:16-17).

The law is not of faith; but, The man that doeth them shall live in them (Gal. 3:12).

5. HOW MAN SINNED

13. Did our first parents continue in the estate wherein they were created?

A.   Our first parents, being left to the freedom of their own will, fell from the estate wherein they were created, by *sinning against God*.

Comment

Adam and Eve did not keep God's command. They sought to please themselves instead of seeking to please God, and so they fell from a state of innocence into a state of sin.

Proofs

I call heaven and earth to record this day against you, that I have set before you life and death, blessing and cursing; therefore choose life, that both thou and thy seed may live (Deut. 30:19).

And when the woman saw that the tree was good for food, and that it was pleasant to the eyes, and a tree to be desired to make one wise, she took of the fruit thereof, and did eat, and gave also unto her husband with her; and he did eat (Gen. 3:6).

14. What is sin?

A. Sin is *any want of conformity* unto, or *transgression* of, the Law of God.

Comment

We are here taught that there are two kinds of sins. The first consists in not doing what God commands; the second consists in doing what God forbids. Our first parents committed the latter.

Proofs

And by chance there came down a certain priest that way; and when he saw him, he passed by on the other side (Luke 10:31).

And the Lord turned, and looked upon Peter. And Peter remembered the word of the Lord, how he had said unto him, Before the cock crow thou shalt deny me thrice (Luke 22:61).

15. What was the sin whereby our first parents fell from the estate wherein they were created?

A.   The sin whereby our first parents fell from
     the estate wherein they were created, was
     their eating the forbidden fruit.

Comment
The particular sin which Adam and Eve committed,
and which constituted their fall, consisted in their
eating of the tree of the knowledge of good and evil,
of which God had said they should not eat.

Proof
  She took of the fruit thereof, and did eat, and
  gave also unto her husband with her; and he did
  eat (Gen. 3:6).

6. CONSEQUENCES OF MAN'S SIN

16. **Did all mankind fall in Adam's first
     transgression?**

A.   The covenant being made with Adam,
     not only for himself, but for his posterity;
     all mankind – descending from him by
     ordinary generation – *sinned in him*, and *fell
     with him*, in his first transgression.

Comment

The agreement which God made with Adam did not affect himself alone, but all his descendants. When Adam sinned, therefore, the whole of the human race, except Christ, incurred along with him his punishment – the punishment of death. They 'sinned in him and fell in him'. This result is in strict keeping with the plan on which all the world's affairs are conducted, for we still see children suffering on account of the misdeeds of their parents.

Proofs

By the offence of one judgment came upon all men to condemnation ... By one man's disobedience many were made sinners (Rom. 5:18-19).

As in Adam all die, even so in Christ shall all be made alive (1 Cor. 15:22).

17. Into what estate did the Fall bring mankind?

A.   The Fall brought mankind into an estate of sin and misery.

Comment

Adam's first sin is commonly called the Fall. And we are here told that, in consequence of this Fall, all men are now born in a sinful and unhappy condition.

Proof

By one man sin entered into the world, and death by sin; and so death passed upon all men, for that all have sinned (Rom 5:12).

18. Wherein consists the sinfulness of that estate whereinto man fell?

A. The sinfulness of that estate whereinto man fell consists in the guilt of Adam's first sin, the want of original righteousness, and the *corruption* of his whole nature, which is commonly called original sin; together with all *actual transgressions* which proceed from it.

Comment

This answer tells us of the *extent of the sinfulness* which has been brought upon us through Adam's fall. It tells us that this sinfulness consists of two parts – the sin of our natures, and the sin of our lives. The former is called original sin, and includes these three things: liability to punishment for Adam's sin, want of a desire to do right, and a positive inclination to do wrong. The latter includes all the actual sins we commit. Original sin springs directly from our connexion with Adam.

Actual sin springs directly from our own evil hearts; but then these hearts were made evil at first through our connexion with Adam, so that all sin is really to be traced up to the first one.

Proofs

But I see another law in my members, warring against the law of my mind, and bringing me into captivity to the law of sin which is in my members (Rom. 7:23).

For out of the heart proceed evil thoughts, murders, adulteries, fornications, thefts, false witness, blasphemies (Matt. 15:19).

Behold, I was shapen in iniquity; and in sin did my mother conceive me (Ps. 51:5).

19. **What is the misery of that estate wherein man fell?**

A. All mankind by their fall lost communion with God, are under his *wrath and curse*, and so made liable to *all miseries in this life*, to death itself, and to the pains of *hell* for ever.

Comment

We are here taught the extent of the misery which has come upon us through Adam's sin. We are told that we have, in consequence, no longer that intercourse with God which Adam enjoyed, but are living under his displeasure, and therefore exposed to all the sorrows of this life, the pangs of death, and the pains of hell for ever. This is the condition in which we all are by nature; and, unless God had taken pity on us, this is the condition in which we should all have remained.

Proofs

But your iniquities have separated between you and your God, and your sins have hid his face from you, that he will not hear (Isa. 59:2).

The soul that sinneth, it shall die (Ezek. 18:4).

And unto Adam he said: Because thou hast hearkened unto the voice of thy wife, and hast eaten of the tree, of which I commanded thee, saying: Thou shalt not eat of it: cursed is the ground for thy sake; in sorrow shalt thou eat of it all the days of thy life (Gen. 3:17).

The wicked shall be turned into hell, and all the nations that forget God (Ps. 9:17).

7. SALVATION

20. **Did God leave all mankind to perish in the estate of sin and misery?**

A.   God having, out of his mere good pleasure, from all eternity, elected some to everlasting life, did enter into a covenant of grace, to *deliver them* out of the estate of sin and misery, and to bring them into an estate of *salvation* by a Redeemer.

Comment

Man did not obey God's law, and so he was condemned to death, both of body and of soul. But it was not the will of God that the world should perish, and so there was another covenant made, but this time with Christ, called the Covenant of Grace, by which God undertook to deliver those who should believe in his Son, and give them everlasting life. This is the Gospel, or Good News of God to men; and it is called the Covenant of Grace, because it proceeded from God's free mercy, and not from our deservings.

Proofs

And I will put enmity between thee and the
woman, and between thy seed and her seed; it
shall bruise thy head, and thou shalt bruise his
heel *(*Gen. 3:15).

Who hath saved us, and called us with an holy
calling, not according to our works, but according
to his own purpose and grace, which was given us
in Christ Jesus before the world began (2 Tim. 1:9).

21. Who is the Redeemer of God's elect?

A.   The only redeemer of God's elect is the
Lord Jesus Christ, who, being the eternal
Son of God, **became man**, and so was,
and continueth to be, *God and man* in two
distinct natures, and one person, for ever.

Comment

To *redeem* is to *buy back* something which has been
possessed before, but of which the possession has been
lost. Now, Jesus Christ redeemed us with his own
blood. And of this Redeemer we are here told that,
being God, he became man; so that the two natures
in him remain henceforth and for ever united in one
person. Jesus Christ, we must remember therefore,

is not something *between* God and man, but *both* God and man.

Proofs

Neither is there salvation in any other: for there is none other name under heaven given among men, whereby we must be saved (Acts 4:12).

Forasmuch then as the children are partakers of flesh and blood, he also himself likewise took part of the same; that through death he might destroy him that had the power of death, that is, the devil (Heb. 2:14).

I am he that liveth, and was dead; and behold, I am alive for evermore, Amen; and have the keys of hell and of death (Rev. 1:18).

22. **How did Christ, being the Son of God, become man?**

A.   Christ, the Son of God, became man, by taking to himself a true body, and a reasonable soul, being conceived by the power of the *Holy Ghost*, in the womb of the *Virgin Mary*, and born of her, yet without sin.

Comment

The last answer told us the fact that the Son of God became man; this answer tells us how he did so. He did so by assuming a human body and soul. And this was assumed in a miraculous manner, through the power of the Holy Spirit. The purpose for which Christ became man was that he might stand in our place and work out our redemption.

Proofs

And the angel answered and said unto her: The Holy Ghost shall come upon thee, and the power of the Highest shall overshadow thee; therefore also that holy thing which shall be born of thee shall be called the Son of God (Luke 1:35).

But when the fulness of the time was come, God sent forth his Son, made of a woman, made under the law (Gal. 4:4).

For such an high priest became us, who is holy, harmless, undefiled, separate from sinners, and made higher than the heavens (Heb. 7:26).

8. CHRIST'S WORK IN SALVATION

23.   What offices doth Christ execute as our Redeemer?

A.   Christ, as our Redeemer, executeth the offices of a prophet, of a priest, and of a king, both in his estate of *humiliation* and *exaltation*.

Comment

In the last section we were taught the great truth that sinners may be saved. In this section we are taught the *way* in which our Redeemer works out salvation to his people.

He does so, we are told, by discharging the duties of a prophet, a priest, and a king, and thereby delivering us from our threefold misery of ignorance, guilt, and bondage. He performed these duties while he was here on earth, and he still continues to perform them in heaven.

Proofs

For Moses truly said unto the fathers: A prophet shall the Lord your God raise up unto you of your brethren, like unto me; him shall ye hear in all things whatsoever he shall say unto you (Acts 3:22).

As he saith also in another place: Thou art a priest for ever after the order of Melchisedec (Heb. 5:6).

Yet have I set my king upon my holy hill of Zion (Ps. 2:6).

24. How doth Christ execute the office of a prophet?

A.   Christ executeth the office of a prophet, in *revealing* to us, by his Word and Spirit, the will of God for our salvation.

Comment

A prophet is a man who declares the will of God; and we are here told that this is what Christ, as our prophet, does for us. He does so by his Word, for the whole Bible is his; but inasmuch as the mere reading of the Bible is not sufficient of itself to make a man wise unto salvation, he likewise bestows his *Holy Spirit*, that so the Word may profit those who hear it.

Proofs

God, who at sundry times and in divers manners spake in time past unto the fathers by the prophets, hath in these last days spoken unto us by his Son, whom he hath appointed heir of all things, by whom also he made the worlds (Heb. 1:1, 2).

Howbeit when he, the Spirit of truth, is come, he
will guide you into all truth; for he shall not speak
of himself; but whatsoever he shall hear, that shall
he speak; and he will show you things to come
(John 16:13).

25. **How doth Christ execute the office of a
     priest?**

A.   Christ executeth the office of a priest, in
     his once *offering up of himself* a **sacrifice**,
     to satisfy Divine justice, and reconcile us
     to God; and in *making continual intercession*
     for us.

Comment

The duties of a priest were to offer sacrifices and pray
for the people; and this is what Christ, as our priest,
does for us. When he was here on earth, he offered
himself as a sacrifice; and now that he is in heaven,
he intercedes for us with his Father. We are here told,
likewise, that the purposes for which Christ offered
himself as a sacrifice were: 1. To satisfy the justice of
God on account of our sin; and 2. To bring us back
to God as dear children.

Proofs

We have a great high priest, that is passed into the heavens, Jesus the Son of God (Heb. 4:14).

Christ was once offered to bear the sins of many (Heb. 9:28).

And, having made peace through the blood of his cross, by him to reconcile all things unto himself; by him, I say, whether they be things in earth, or things in heaven (Col. 1:20).

Wherefore he is able also to save them to the uttermost that come unto God by him, seeing he ever liveth to make intercession for them (Heb. 7:25).

26. **How doth Christ execute the office of a king?**

A. Christ executeth the office of a king, in **subduing us to himself**, in *ruling and defending* us, and in *restraining and conquering* all his and our enemies.

Comment

A king is the ruler of a kingdom. Now there is a great kingdom set up on earth, consisting of all God's people, and its ruler is Christ. As such, his duties are here said

to be threefold: 1. He makes us willing to obey him;
2. He gives us laws for our guidance and safety; 3. He
limits and finally puts down all who oppose us and him.

Proofs

Casting down imaginations, and every high thing
that exalteth itself against the knowledge of God,
and bringing into captivity every thought to the
obedience of Christ (2 Cor. 10:5).

Take my yoke upon you, and learn of me; for I
am meek and lowly in heart; and ye shall find rest
unto your souls (Matt. 11:29).

And the Lord shall deliver me from every evil
work, and will preserve me unto his heavenly
kingdom; to whom be glory for ever and ever
(2 Tim. 4:18).

27. Wherein did Christ's humiliation consist?

A.   Christ's humiliation consisted in his *being
born* and that in *a low condition*, made *under
the law*, undergoing the *miseries of this life*,
the *wrath of God*, and the cursed death of
the cross; in being *buried*, and *continuing
under the power of death* for a time.

Comment

Humiliation means coming down from a high rank to a low. Christ did so for us. He descended from his throne in heaven, and became a man of sorrows and acquainted with grief. In this answer we are told the various particulars in which his humiliation consisted. It consisted: 1. In being born; 2. In being born poor; 3. In being subject to the law; 4. In suffering the sorrows of life; 5. In suffering the hiding of God's countenance; 6. In being crucified; 7. In being buried; 8. In remaining in the grave for three days. All these things were borne by Christ, and on our behalf.

Proofs

And she brought forth her firstborn son and wrapped him in swaddling clothes, and laid him in a manger (Luke 2:7).

And about the ninth hour Jesus cried with a loud voice, saying, Eli! Eli! Lama sabachthani? That is to say, My God! My God! Why hast thou forsaken me? (Matt. 27:46).

Who, being in the form of God, thought it not robbery to be equal with God; but made himself of no reputation, and took upon him the form of a servant, and was made in the likeness of men: and being found in fashion as a man, he humbled himself, and became obedient unto death, even the death of the cross (Phil. 2:6-8).

For as Jonah was three days and three nights in the whale's belly, so shall the Son of man be three days and three nights in the heart of the earth (Matt. 12:40).

28. Wherein consisteth Christ's exaltation?

A.   Christ's exaltation consisteth in his *rising again from the dead* on the third day, in ascending up into heaven, in **sitting at the right hand of God** the *Father*, and in *coming to judge the world* at the last day.

Comment

Exaltation means a rising from meanness to greatness. Christ's exaltation consists in the following particulars: 1. In rising from the dead; 2. In ascending up into heaven; 3. In sitting at God's right hand; 4. In being appointed to judge the world. This is the state in which our Saviour is now.

Proofs

He is not here; for he is risen, as he said. Come see the place where the Lord lay (Matt. 28:6).

He was received up into heaven, and sat on the right hand of God (Mark 16:19).

When the Son of man shall come in his glory, and all the holy angels with him, then shall he sit upon the throne of his glory: And before him shall be gathered all nations; and he shall separate them one from another, as a shepherd divideth his sheep from the goats (Matt. 25:31, 32).

9. THE SPIRIT'S WORK IN SALVATION

29. **How are we made partakers of the redemption purchased by Christ?**

A.   We are made partakers of the redemption purchased by Christ, by the *effectual application* of it to us by his Holy Spirit.

Comment

Having seen, in the previous section, how salvation has been brought within our reach, we now come to learn the way in which we may become possessed of it. In this answer we are told, that while it is Christ who has purchased redemption for us, it is the Holy Spirit who puts us actually in possession of it.

Proofs

When he, the Spirit of truth, is come, he will guide you into all truth (John 16:13).

As many as are led by the Spirit of God, they are the sons of God (Rom. 8:14).

30. How doth the Spirit apply to us the redemption purchased by Christ?

A.   The Spirit applieth to us the redemption purchased by Christ, by working faith in us, and thereby *uniting us to Christ* in our effectual calling.

Comment

The last answer tells us *by whose* agency we become possessed of salvation; this one tells us of the method of it. It tells us that Christ's salvation becomes ours by union with him – that we are united to him by faith – and that this faith by which we commit ourselves to Christ, is the effect of the working of God's Spirit in our hearts. Faith in Christ means *trust* in Christ, and brings about *union* with him.

Proofs

When the Comforter is come ... he shall testify of me (John 15:26).

No man can say that Jesus is the Lord, but by the Holy Ghost (1 Cor. 12:3).

I am the vine, ye are the branches; he that abideth in me, and I in him, the same bringeth forth much fruit; for without me ye can do nothing (John 15:5).

31. What is effectual calling?

A.   Effectual calling is the work of God's Spirit, whereby, convincing us of our *sin and misery*, enlightening our minds in the *knowledge of Christ*, and *renewing our wills*, he doth persuade and enable us to *embrace* Jesus Christ, freely offered to us in the Gospel.

Comment

There are two ways by which God calls or invites men to be saved – the *outward* call of his Word or his Providence, and the *inward* call of his Spirit. The former of these is often ineffectual through the evil of our hearts; the latter is always effectual. The steps or stages of the *inward, effectual* call of the Spirit are four: 1. *Conviction*, or making us feel our sin; 2. *Enlightenment*, or making the way of salvation plain to us; 3. *Renewal*, or inclining us anew to the love and practice of what is good and right; and 4. As the fruit of these, *Faith*, or enabling us to trust in Jesus Christ as our Saviour.

Proofs

When the Comforter is come, he will reprove the world of sin, and of righteousness, and of judgment (John 16:8).

That the God of our Lord Jesus Christ, the Father of glory, may give unto you the spirit of wisdom and revelation in the knowledge of him (Eph. 1:17).

For they that are after the flesh do mind the things of the flesh; but they that are after the Spirit the things of the Spirit (Rom. 8:5).

No man can come to me, except the Father which hath sent me draw him ... Every man therefore that hath heard, and hath learned of the Father, cometh unto me (John 6:44, 45).

10. THE BENEFITS OF SALVATION IN THIS LIFE

32. **What benefits do they that are effectually called partake of in this life?**

A. They that are effectually called do in this life partake of **justification, adoption** and **sanctification**, and the *several benefits* which, in this life, do either accompany or flow from them.

Comment

Faith in Christ insures certain blessings, some of which are enjoyed in this life, others in the world to come. Of those enjoyed in this life, justification, adoption, and sanctification are the chief, and are of such a nature as to hold within them, or bring along with them, every other blessing.

Proofs

But of him are ye in Christ Jesus, who of God is made unto us wisdom, and righteousness, and sanctification, and redemption (1 Cor 1:30).

Moreover, whom he did predestinate, them he also called; and whom he called, them he also justified;

and whom he justified, them he also glorified
(Rom 8:30).

33. What is justification?

A.   Justification is an *act of God's free grace*,
      wherein he *pardoneth all our sins*, and *accepteth
      us as righteous* in his sight, only for the
      righteousness of Christ imputed to us,
      and received by *faith* alone.

Comment

Justification means pronouncing a person righteous; it is
the opposite of *condemnation*. It is said to be an *act*, because
it is done at once; and an act of God's *free grace*, because we
can do nothing of ourselves to deserve it. It consists of two
parts – *pardon* and *acceptance*; and we are taught also that
the *cause* of it is not our own goodness, but *Christ's*, and
that Christ's righteousness becomes ours through *faith*.

Proofs

Being justified freely by his grace through the
redemption that is in Christ Jesus (Rom. 3:24).

In whom we have redemption through his blood,
the forgiveness of sins, according to the riches of
his grace (Eph. 1:7).

For as by one man's disobedience many were made
sinners, so by the obedience of one shall many be
made righteous (Rom. 5:19).

A man is not justified by the works of the law, but
by the faith of Jesus Christ (Gal. 2:16).

34. What is adoption?

A.   *Adoption* is an *act of God's free grace*, whereby
     we are *received into the number* – and *have a
     right to all the privileges* – of the sons of God.

Comment

Adoption denotes the taking of a child who is a stranger
into a family, and treating him as a member of it. Such
is the adoption meant here. It too, like justification,
is an act of pure favour on God's part, and confers
blessings to which we had lost all claim. It confers
upon us both the *rank* and *rights* of children, and
makes us feel that we have both a *place* and a *portion as
sons* in God's family.

Proofs

Behold what manner of love the Father hath
bestowed upon us, that we should be called the
sons of God (1 John 3:1).

And if children, then heirs; heirs of God, and joint-heirs with Christ (Rom. 8:17).

35. **What is sanctification?**

A. Sanctification is *the work of God's free grace*, whereby we are renewed in the whole man after the **image of God**, and are enabled more and more to *die unto sin*, and *live unto righteousness*.

Comment

Sanctification means making a person holy. It is here said to be a *work*, because it is done, not at once, but gradually; and a work of *grace* because it proceeds from God's undeserved goodness, and is wrought in us from first to last by his own Spirit. It consists in our being made *like to God* – that is, in gradually learning to hate and cease from sin, and to love and practise holiness; and this is called a *renewing*, because it is restoring us to the state in which we were at first.

Justification, adoption and sanctification are thus seen to be all necessary to salvation. In justification, the sinner is pardoned; in adoption, he is brought into the family; in sanctification, he is cleansed from all sin.

Proofs

Not by works of righteousness which we have done, but according to his mercy he saved us, by the washing of regeneration, and renewing of the Holy Ghost (Titus 3:5).

Put on the new man, which after God is created in righteousness and true holiness (Eph. 4:24).

Brethren, I count not myself to have apprehended: but this one thing I do, forgetting those things which are behind, and reaching forth unto those things which are before, I press toward the mark for the prize of the high calling of God in Christ Jesus (Phil. 3:13, 14).

But the path of the just is as the shining light, that shineth more and more unto the perfect day (Prov. 4:18).

36. **What are the benefits which in this life do accompany or flow from justification, adoption, and sanctification?**

A. The benefits which in this life do accompany or flow from justification, adoption, and sanctification, are, *assurance of God's love, peace of conscience, joy in the Holy Ghost, increase of grace*, and *perseverance* therein to the end.

Comment

Here are five blessings enumerated for us, which, in this life, necessarily either go along with or flow from the three just described. They who are justified, adopted, and are being sanctified, enjoy for that reason: 1. Confidence that God loves them; 2. Freedom from the sense of guilt and fear of condemnation; 3. Gladness of heart in feeling that the Holy Spirit is dwelling in them; 4. A greater and greater increase of spiritual endowment; 5. The power of persevering in the enjoyment of all these graces to the end.

Proofs

And we have known and believed the love that God hath to us (1 John 4:16).

Therefore being justified by faith, we have peace with God, through our Lord Jesus Christ: By whom also we have access by faith into this grace wherein we stand, and rejoice in hope of the glory of God (Rom. 5:1, 2).

Now the God of hope fill you with all joy and peace in believing, that ye may abound in hope, through the power of the Holy Ghost (Rom. 15:13).

Being confident of this very thing, that he which hath begun a good work in you will perform it until the day of Jesus Christ (Phil. 1:6).

11. THE BENEFITS OF SALVATION AFTER THIS LIFE

37.   What benefits do believers receive from Christ at death?

A   The souls of believers are at their death made *perfect in holiness*, and do immediately **pass into Glory**; and their *bodies*, being still *united to Christ*, do rest in their graves till the resurrection.

Comment

Having learned the blessings which true Christians receive from God in this life, we are now taught the blessings they receive when this life is ended. 1. The *soul* is then made perfectly holy, or free from all sinful tendencies, and taken at once to heaven; 2. The *body* rests in the grave in union with Christ till the last day.

Proofs

And there shall in no wise enter into it any thing that defileth, neither whatsoever worketh abomination, or maketh a lie; but they which are written in the Lamb's book of life (Rev. 21:27).

And Jesus said unto him, Verily, I say unto thee, Today shalt thou be with me in paradise (Luke 23:43).

For if we believe that Jesus died and rose again, even so them also which sleep in Jesus will God bring with him (1 Thess. 4:14).

38. What benefits do believers receive from Christ at the resurrection?

A. At the resurrection, believers being *raised up in glory*, shall be *openly acknowledged and acquitted* in the day of judgment, and made perfectly blessed in the full **enjoying** of God to all eternity.

Comment

We are here taught that there will be a resurrection, and after the resurrection a judgment. At that judgment those who have believed in Jesus will be blessed in the following ways: 1. They will be raised up with glorified bodies; 2. They will be acknowledged by Christ, the Judge, as his own people, and declared free from all guilt before an assembled world; 3. They will be taken to heaven, where they shall be happy with God for ever.

Proofs

It is sown in dishonour; it is raised in glory; it is sown in weakness; it is raised in power (1 Cor. 15:43).

Then shall the King say unto them on his right hand, Come, ye blessed of my Father, inherit the kingdom prepared for you from the foundation of the world (Matt. 25:34).

And God shall wipe away all tears from their eyes; and there shall be no more death, neither sorrow, nor crying, neither shall there be any more pain: for the former things are passed away (Rev. 21:4).

So shall we ever be with the Lord (1 Thess. 4:17).

DIVISION 2:
WHAT WE ARE TO DO

1. THE MORAL LAW

39.   What is the duty which God requireth of man?

A.   The duty which God requireth of man, is obedience to His revealed will.

Comment

Having just learned what God has done, is doing, and means to do for us, we are now to be told what he requires us to do *for him*. What he requires of us is *obedience* to all that he reveals. This is our *duty*, or *what we ought to do*.

Proofs

Fear God, and keep his commandments: for this is the whole duty of man (Eccles. 12:13).

He hath showed thee, O man, what is good; and what doth the LORD require of thee but to do justly, and to love mercy, and to walk humbly with thy God? (Micah 6:8).

40.   What did God at first reveal to man for the rule of his obedience?

A.   The rule which God at first revealed to man for his obedience, was **the Moral Law**.

Proof

For when the Gentiles, which have not the law, do by nature the things contained in the law, these, not having the law, are a law unto themselves (Rom. 2:14).

41.   Where is the Moral Law summarily comprehended?

A.   The Moral Law is summarily comprehended in **the Ten Commandments**.

Comment

The Moral Law is the law which teaches us how we ought to think and act with regard to God and man. When God created man, he set this Moral Law in his heart, so that he knew his duty without a Bible. But when man sinned, this knowledge was partly lost, and God therefore had to give it anew. He gave it fully in the Bible, and briefly in the Ten Commandments.

Proofs

And he wrote on the tablets, according to the first writing, the ten commandments, which the LORD spake unto you in the mount, out of the midst of the fire, in the day of the assembly (Deut. 10:4).

If thou wilt enter into life, keep the commandments (Matt. 9:17).

42. What is the sum of the Ten Commandments?

A. The sum of the Ten Commandments is, **to love the Lord our God** with all our heart, with all our soul, with all our strength, and with all our mind; and **our neighbour** as ourselves.

Comment

The whole of God's commands to us are here summed up in one word – love. The man who with his whole soul loves God and his neighbour, fulfils the law. *Neighbour* here means not merely one who lives near us, but, as Christ teaches us (Luke 10), whoever holds kindred with us, or is a man.

Proofs

Jesus said unto him, Thou shalt love the Lord thy God with all thy heart, and with all thy soul, and with all thy mind ... Thou shalt love thy neighbour as thyself. On these two commandments hang all the law and the prophets (Matt. 22:37, 39, 40).

Love is the fulfilling of the law (Rom. 13:10).

43. What is the preface to the Ten Commandments?

A.   The preface to the Ten Commandments is in these words, **'I am the Lord thy God, which have brought thee out of the land of Egypt, out of the House of Bondage.'**

Comment

These are the words which precede the Ten Commandments. They were spoken to the children of Israel at Mount Sinai, shortly after their deliverance from the bondage of the Egyptians (Exod. 20:2). And they may be applied to us in token of our deliverance from the bondage of sin.

44. What doth the preface to the Ten Commandments teach us?

A.   The preface to the Ten Commandments teacheth us, That because God is **the Lord**, and **our God**, and **Redeemer**, therefore we are bound to keep all his commandments.

Comment

The preface to the Ten Commandments sets forth God's claims to obedience at our hands. These are: 1. God is our Sovereign – **I am the Lord**. 2. He is the Being whom we worship – **I am thy God**. 3. He is the One who has delivered us from bondage – **I am Thy Redeemer**.

Proofs

Thou shalt remember that thou wast a bondman in Egypt, and the LORD thy God redeemed thee thence: therefore I command thee to do this thing (Deut. 24:18).

And that he died for all, that they which live should not henceforth live unto themselves, but unto him which died for them, and rose again (2 Cor. 5:15).

FIRST TABLE OF THE LAW

2. THE FIRST COMMANDMENT

45.   Which is the First Commandment?

A.   The First Commandment is, **Thou shalt have no other Gods before me.**

Comment

God wrote the Ten Commandments on two tables of stone. On the first table he wrote the first four commandments, which contain our duty to God; and on the second he wrote the remaining six commandments, which contain our duty to man. This First Commandment teaches us the only proper *object* of worship. It is **God** – and beside him there is no other. This is the simple meaning of the commandment, but in the *Shorter Catechism* each commandment is explained and expanded, by showing first what it *bids* us do, than what it *forbids* us to do, and, lastly, what *special reasons* or motives there may be for its observance.

46.   What is required in the First Commandment?

A.   The First Commandment requireth us to *know* and *acknowledge* God to be the only *true* God, and *our* God; and to *worship* and *glorify* him accordingly.

Comment

The First Commandment bids us – 1. Know the true God, and him only for *our* God; 2. As such confess him openly before men; 3. Worship him; 4. Honour him.

Proofs

And thou, Solomon my son, know thou the God of thy father, and serve him with a perfect heart, and with a willing mind: for the LORD searcheth all hearts, and understandeth all the imagination of the thoughts: if thou seek him he will be found of thee: but if thou forsake him, he will cast thee off for ever (1 Chron. 28:9).

In all thy ways acknowledge him, and he shall direct thy paths (Prov. 3:6).

47. **What is forbidden in the First Commandment?**

A.   The First Commandment forbiddeth the *denying*, or *not worshipping and glorifying* the true God, as God, and our God; and the giving of that worship and glory *to any other* which is due to him alone.

Comment

The First Commandment forbids us: 1. To deny God, which is *atheism*; 2. To worship any other God, which is *idolatry*; 3. To glorify any other God, which is *profanity*.

Proofs

The fool hath said in his heart, There is no God (Ps. 14:1).

Then saith Jesus unto him, Get thee hence, Satan: for it is written, Thou shalt worship the Lord thy God, and him only shalt thou serve (Matt. 4:10).

Who changed the truth of God into a lie, and worshipped and served the creature more than the Creator, who is blessed for ever. Amen (Rom. 1:25).

48. **What are we specially taught by these words, 'before me', in the First Commandment?**

A.   These words – 'before me' – in the First Commandment, teach us, That God who seeth all things, *taketh notice of*, and is *much displeased with*, the sin of **having any other God**.

Comment

The special reason here given why we should observe this commandment is, that God, who seeth all things, keeps an eye especially on the breaking of this commandment, and punishes the offence with his sorest displeasure.

Proofs

If we have forgotten the name of our God, or stretched out our hands to a strange god; shall not God search this out? For he knoweth the secrets of the heart (Ps. 44:20, 21).

They are without excuse: because that, when they knew God, they glorified him not as God (Rom. 1:20, 21).

3. THE SECOND COMMANDMENT

49. Which is the Second Commandment?

A. The Second Commandment is, **thou shalt not make unto thee any graven image**, or any likeness of any thing that is in heaven above, or that is in the earth beneath, or

that is in the water under the earth, **thou
shalt not bow down thyself to them,
nor serve them**: for I the LORD thy God
am a *jealous* God, visiting the iniquity
of the fathers upon the children, unto
the third and fourth generation of them
that hate me; and showing mercy unto
thousands of them that love me, and keep
my commandments.

Comment

The First Commandment tells us whom we are to
worship. The Second tells us how we are to worship
him. It tells us we must not think to represent
God to our minds by any image visible or even
conceivable, or that he will accept such worship at
our hands. We must worship God, who is a Spirit,
in spirit and in truth. We are here likewise told
that God visits the iniquity of the fathers upon the
children; but this does not mean that the children
have to bear the *guilt* of the fathers. It means only
that bad fathers are punished by seeing the evils
of their misconduct entailed upon their children,
while good fathers are cheered and rewarded by
the opposite.

50. What is required in the Second Commandment?

A. The Second Commandment requireth the receiving, observing, and keeping pure and entire, *all such religious worship and ordinances as God hath appointed* in his Word.

Comment

This commandment bids us: 1. Adopt the way of worshipping God appointed by himself; 2. Adhere to it; 3. Not add to it; 4. Nor take from it. There must be no will-worship.

Proofs

Teaching them to observe all things whatsoever I have commanded you (Matt. 28:20).

What thing soever I command you, observe to do it: thou shalt not add thereto, nor diminish from it (Deut. 12:32).

51. What is forbidden in the Second Commandment?

A. The Second Commandment forbiddeth the worshipping of God by *images – or any other way not appointed in his Word*.

Comment

This command forbids us: 1. To make use of images in worship; 2. To make use of any other means than those God has appointed.

Proofs

Take ye therefore good heed unto yourselves; for ye saw no manner of similitude on the day that the LORD spake unto you in Horeb out of the midst of the fire (Deut. 4:15).

But in vain do they worship me, teaching for doctrines the commandments of men (Matt. 15:9).

52. What are the reasons annexed to the Second Commandment?

A. The reasons annexed to the Second Commandment are, God's *sovereignty* over us, his *propriety* in us, and the *zeal* he hath to his own worship.

Comment

The special reasons added why we should observe this commandment are: 1. God is our Sovereign (I, the Lord); 2. God is our owner (thy God); 3. God is zealous for his own worship (am a jealous God).

Proofs

For the LORD is a great God, and a great King above all gods (Ps. 95:3).

For thou shalt worship no other god: for the LORD, whose name is Jealous, is a jealous God (Exod. 34:14).

4. THE THIRD COMMANDMENT

53. Which is the Third Commandment?

A. The Third Commandment is, thou shalt not take the name of the Lord thy God in vain: for the LORD will not hold him guiltless that taketh his name in vain.

Comment

This commandment tells how to treat the Name of God, and by his *Name* is meant everything by which he is named to us, or specially made known. To take God's name in vain is to use it for a vain or frivolous purpose; and we break this command by profane swearing, or by irreverently using God's name. We recognise the command when we pray – *Hallowed be thy Name.*

54. What is required in the Third Commandment?

A. The Third Commandment requireth *the holy and reverent use* of God's name, titles, attributes, ordinances, Word, and works

Comment

The Third Commandment bids us use in very reverent manner – 1. God's names, such as *the Lord*; 2. His titles, such as *King of Kings*; 3. His attributes, such as *holiness*; 4. His ordinances, such as *prayer*; 5. His Word, or *the Bible*; 6. His works, such as *man*.

Proofs

Give unto the LORD the glory due unto his name; worship the LORD in the beauty of holiness (Ps. 29:2).

Keep thy foot when thou goest to the house of God, and be more ready to hear than to give the sacrifice of fools: for they consider not that they do evil (Eccles. 5:1).

Remember that thou magnify his work, which men behold (Job 36:24).

55. What is forbidden in the Third Commandment?

A. The Third Commandment forbiddeth all *profaning* or *abusing* of anything whereby God maketh himself known.

Comment
The Third Commandment forbids us to use irreverently or wrongly any of the names or things which more especially express and declare God. Everything connected with *him* should be sacred.

Proof
But I say unto you, Swear not at all: neither by heaven; for it is God's throne: Nor by the earth; for it is his footstool: neither by Jerusalem; for it is the city of the great King (Matt. 5:34, 35).

56. What is the reason annexed to the Third Commandment?

A. The reason annexed to the Third Commandment is, That however the breakers of this commandment may escape punishment from *men*, yet **The Lord our**

God will not suffer them to escape *his* righteous judgment.

Comment

The special warning here held out to us is, that although men may permit us to break this commandment with impunity, yet God will assuredly not do so. *He* will not fail to judge us.

Proofs

If thou wilt not observe to do all the words of this law that are written in this book, that thou mayest fear this glorious and fearful name, The LORD thy God; then the LORD will make thy plagues wonderful (Deut. 28:58, 59).

5. THE FOURTH COMMANDMENT

57. Which is the Fourth Commandment?

A. The Fourth Commandment is, **remember the Sabbath Day, to keep it holy.** *Six days* shalt thou labour, and do all thy work; but the *seventh day* is the **Sabbath** of the LORD thy God: in it **thou shalt not do any work,** thou, nor thy son, nor thy daughter, thy man-servant, nor thy maid-servant, nor thy cattle, nor thy stranger that is within thy gates: for in *six days* the LORD made heaven and earth, the sea, and all that in them is, and *rested the seventh day*: wherefore the LORD *blessed* the Sabbath-day, and *hallowed* it.

Comment

This commandment fixes the *portion of our time* which God requires us and our households to give exclusively to his worship – namely, one day in seven. Six days for *work* – one for *worship*. Such is the division of our time appointed for us by God, and required by the nature he has given us. The word *remember* is used in this commandment as implying that the Sabbath was not instituted here for the first time.

58. What is required in the Fourth Commandment?

A. The Fourth Commandment requireth the keeping holy to God *such set times as he hath appointed in his Word*; expressly *one whole day in seven*, to be a holy Sabbath to himself.

Comment

The Sabbath is an emblem of heaven, and a pattern and example for all days. Every day should be holy unto the Lord. Inasmuch, however, as in this world we must engage in worldly business, the Sabbath was instituted to prevent our thoughts from dwelling too much on worldly matters. It is intended for man's good, and it is our own loss if we disregard it.

Proof

Ye shall keep my sabbaths, and reverence my sanctuary; I am the LORD (Lev. 19:30).

59. Which day of the seven hath God appointed to be the weekly Sabbath?

A.   From the beginning of the world to the resurrection of Christ, God appointed the *seventh* day of the week to be the weekly Sabbath; and the *first* day of the week ever since, to continue to the end of the world, which is the **Christian** Sabbath.

Comment

The Patriarchal and Jewish Sabbath was held on the *Saturday*, because that was the day on which God rested from Creation. The Christian Sabbath is held on the

Sunday, because that is the day on which our Saviour arose from the grave. The change was made in accordance with the practice of the Apostles and the early Church.

Proofs

And God blessed the seventh day, and sanctified it; because that in it he had rested from all his work which God created and made (Gen. 2:3).

And upon the first day of the week, when the disciples came together to break bread, Paul preached unto them (Acts 20:7).

I was in the Spirit on the Lord's day (Rev. 1:10).

60. How is the Sabbath to be sanctified?

A.   The Sabbath is to be sanctified by a holy **resting** all that day, even from such worldly employments and recreations as are lawful on *other* days; and spending the whole time in the *public and private exercises of God's worship*, except so much as is to be taken up in the works of **necessity** and **mercy**.

Comment

This answer teaches us that the proper way of observing the Sabbath is by: 1. Resting from all secular work;

2. Ceasing from amusement; 3. Engaging in public worship; 4. Engaging in private worship. The only kinds of work allowable on the Sabbath are works of *necessity* – that is, such as cannot be done on the Saturday, nor left over till the Monday; and works of *mercy* – that is, such as it would be cruel to omit.

Proofs

Six days shall work be done: but the seventh day is the sabbath of rest, an holy convocation; ye shall do no work therein: it is the sabbath day of the LORD in all your dwellings (Lev. 23:3).

A Psalm or Song for the Sabbath-day. It is a good thing to give thanks unto the LORD, and to sing praises unto thy name, O most High (Ps. 92:1).

And he said unto them, What man shall there be among you that shall have one sheep, and if it fall into a pit on the sabbath day, will he not lay hold on it and lift it out? ... Wherefore it is lawful to do well on the sabbath days (Matt. 12:11, 12).

61. What is forbidden in the Fourth Commandment?

A.   The Fourth Commandment forbiddeth the *omission or careless performance* of the duties required, and the profaning the day by *idleness*, or doing that which is in itself *sinful*, or by unnecessary thoughts, words, or works, about our *worldly* employments or recreations.

Comment

This commandment forbids: 1. The omission of Sabbath duties; 2. The careless discharge of them; 3. Being idle; 4. Committing sin; 5. Being engaged, without proper reason, in worldly matters.

Proofs

If thou turn away thy foot from the sabbath, from doing thy pleasure on my holy day; and call the sabbath a delight, the holy of the LORD, honourable: and shalt honour him, not doing thine own ways, nor finding thine own pleasure, nor speaking thine own words: Then shalt thou delight thyself in the LORD; and I will cause thee to ride upon the high places of the earth, and feed thee with the heritage of Jacob thy father; for the mouth of the LORD hath spoken it (Isa. 58:13, 14).

Ye said also, Behold, what a weariness is it! and ye have snuffed at it, saith the LORD of hosts; and ye brought that which was torn, and the lame, and the sick; thus ye brought an offering: should I accept this of your hand? saith the LORD (Mal. 1:13).

62. What are the reasons annexed to the Fourth Commandment?

A. The reasons annexed to the Fourth Commandment are – God's allowing us *six* days of the week for our own employments; his challenging a special propriety in the *seventh*; his own *example*; and his *blessing* the Sabbath-day.

Comment

The special reasons here given for the observance of the Sabbath are: 1. Our being allowed six days for work; 2. God's claim of the seventh day as specially his own; 3. God's resting on the seventh day; 4. God's blessing it.

Proofs

Six days may work be done; but in the seventh is the sabbath of rest, holy to the LORD: whosoever doeth any work in the sabbath-day, he shall surely be put to death (Exod. 31:15).

And God blessed the seventh day, and sanctified it: because that in it he had rested from all his work, which God created and made (Gen. 2:3).

SECOND TABLE OF THE LAW

6. THE FIFTH COMMANDMENT

63. Which is the Fifth Commandment?

A.   The Fifth Commandment is, **Honour thy Father and thy Mother;** that thy days may be *long* upon the land which the LORD thy God giveth thee.

64. What is required in the Fifth Commandment?

A.   The Fifth Commandment requireth the *preserving the honour*, and *performing the duties*, belonging to *every one* in their several places and relations, as superiors, inferiors, or equals.

Proofs

Children, obey your parents in all things: for this is well-pleasing unto the Lord (Col. 3:20).

Submitting yourselves one to another in the fear of God (Eph. 5:21).

65. What is forbidden in the Fifth Commandment?

A. The Fifth Commandment forbiddeth the *neglecting of*, or *doing anything against*, the honour and duty which belongeth to every one in their several places and relations.

Proofs

Render therefore to all their dues; tribute to whom tribute is due; custom to whom custom; fear to whom fear; honour to whom honour (Rom. 13:7).

Be kindly affectioned one to another with brotherly love; in honour preferring one another (Rom. 12:10).

66. What is the reason annexed to the Fifth Commandment?

A. The reason annexed to the Fifth Commandment is *a promise of long life and prosperity* (as far as it shall serve for God's glory and their own good) to all such as keep this commandment.

Proof

Honour thy father and mother; (which is the first
commandment with promise); that it may be well
with thee, and thou mayest live long on the earth
(Eph. 6:2, 3).

Comment

The Fifth Commandment stands at the head of the
second table of the law. It requires us to honour
our parents, to render due respect and obedience
to all who are superior to us, and, in a word, to
pay heed to the claims of those who are *related* to
us in any way.

This commandment bids us always show a certain
respect to those above us in station, and requires
certain duties to be discharged to all, whether above,
beneath, or equal to us. It forbids us to refuse to pay
honour to whom honour is due, or to neglect to
discharge any of the duties we owe to our friends
or neighbours. The special reason it gives for its
observance is that God has promised to lengthen the
days of those who keep it.

7. THE SIXTH COMMANDMENT

67. Which is the Sixth Commandment?

A.   The Sixth Commandment is, **Thou shalt not kill.**

68.   **What is required in the Sixth Commandment?**

A.   The Sixth Commandment requireth all lawful endeavours to *preserve* our own life, and the life of others.

Proofs

And he said unto them, Come ye yourselves apart into a desert place, and rest awhile; for there were many coming and going, and they had no leisure so much as to eat (Mark 6:31).

Defend the poor and fatherless: deliver the poor and needy (Ps. 82:3, 4).

69.   **What is forbidden in the Sixth Commandment?**

A.   The Sixth Commandment forbiddeth the *taking away* of our own life, or the life of our neighbour unjustly, or whatsoever *tendeth* thereunto.

Proofs

Paul cried with a loud voice, saying, Do thyself no harm (Acts 16:28).

But I say unto you, That whosoever is angry with his brother without a cause shall be in danger of the judgment; and whosoever shall say to his brother, Raca, shall be in danger of the council; but whosoever shall say, Thou fool, shall be in danger of hell fire (Matt. 5:22).

Comment

This commandment respects *life*. It acknowledges that God is its Giver, and that therefore no one has a right to take it away without just reason.

It commands us to take all proper care of our health, as well as of the health of others. And it forbids us to take away our own life – which is *suicide*; or the life of another – which is *murder*.

8. THE SEVENTH COMMANDMENT

70. Which is the Seventh Commandment?

A.   The Seventh Commandment is, Thou shalt not commit adultery.

71. What is required in the Seventh Commandment?

A.   The Seventh Commandment requireth the preservation of our own and our neighbour's *chastity*, in heart, speech, and behaviour.

Proofs

Flee also youthful lusts: but follow righteousness, faith, charity, peace, with them that call on the Lord out of a pure heart (2 Tim. 2:22).

Have no fellowship with the unfruitful works of darkness, but rather reprove them. For it is a shame even to speak of those things which are done of them in secret (Eph. 5:11,12).

72. What is forbidden in the Seventh Commandment?

A.   The Seventh Commandment forbiddeth *all unchaste* thoughts, words, and actions.

Proofs

But I say unto you, That whosoever looketh on a woman to lust after her hath committed adultery with her already in his heart (Matt. 5:28).

Neither filthiness, nor foolish talking, nor jesting, which are not convenient (Eph. 5:4).

Comment

This commandment respects *purity*. It commands us to be pure in thought, word and deed. It forbids all unchastity and immodesty. It acknowledges God as the owner of the body as well as of the soul, and the right he has to command that both of them should be kept pure and holy for himself.

9. THE EIGHTH COMMANDMENT

73. Which is the Eighth Commandment?

A. The Eighth Commandment is, Thou shalt not steal.

74. What is required in the Eighth Commandment?

A. The Eighth Commandment requireth the *lawful procuring and furthering* the wealth and outward estate of our-selves and others.

Proofs

Provide things honest in the sight of all men (Rom. 12:17).

Let him that stole steal no more: but rather let him
labour, working with his hands the thing which is
good, that he may have to give to him that needeth
(Eph. 4:28).

75. What is forbidden in the Eighth Commandment?

A.   The Eighth Commandment forbiddeth whatsoever doth or may unjustly *hinder* our own
or our neighbour's wealth or outward estate.

Proofs

He that followeth after vain persons shall have
poverty enough (Prov. 28:19).

I have showed you all things, how that so labouring
ye ought to support the weak: and to remember
the words of the Lord Jesus, how he said, It is more
blessed to give than to receive (Acts 20:35).

Comment

This commandment refers to *money* and *property*. It
acknowledges that it is right and proper to gain money,
and that it is wrong in a man to squander his own
property, or to plunder another's. It commands us to
work for the supply of our own needs, and to help

others as well as ourselves to increase in wealth. And it forbids aught that would tend to hinder these ends.

10. THE NINTH COMMANDMENT

76. Which is the Ninth Commandment?

A. The Ninth Commandment is, Thou shalt not bear false witness against thy Neighbour.

77. What is required in the Ninth Commandment?

A. The Ninth Commandment requireth the maintaining and promoting of *truth* between man and man, and of our own and our neighbour's *good name*, especially in witness-bearing.

Proofs

These are things that ye shall do; Speak ye every man the truth to his neighbour: execute the judgment of truth and peace in your gates (Zech. 8:16).

A faithful witness will not lie. A true witness delivereth souls (Prov. 14:5, 25).

78. What is forbidden in the Ninth Commandment?

A.   The Ninth Commandment forbiddeth whatsoever is *prejudicial* to truth, or *injurious* to our own or our neighbour's good name.

Proofs

Let all bitterness, and wrath, and anger, and clamour, and evil speaking, be put away from you, with all malice (Eph. 4:31).

He that backbiteth not with his tongue, nor doeth evil to his neighbour, nor taketh up a reproach against his neighbour (Ps. 15:3).

Comment

This commandment refers to our *words*. It commands us to be careful to speak *the truth* at all times, to stand up for it when it is assailed, and to seek to advance it by all means in our power. And it forbids us to do anything which might make others believe what is not true – which is *lying*; and especially where anyone's character is concerned – which is *slander*. In ordinary intercourse the rule is, Speak the truth in love. In witness-bearing the rule is, Speak the truth, the whole truth and nothing but the truth.

11. THE TENTH COMMANDMENT

79. Which is the Tenth Commandment?

A. The Tenth Commandment is, **Thou shalt not covet** thy neighbour's *house*, thou shalt not covet thy neighbour's *wife*, nor his *man-servant*, nor his *maid-servant*, nor his *ox*, nor his *ass*, nor *any thing* that is thy neighbour's.

80. What is required in the Tenth Commandment?

A. The Tenth Commandment requireth full *contentment* with our own condition, with a *right and charitable frame of spirit* toward our neighbour, and all that is his.

Proofs

And having food and raiment, let us be therewith content (1 Tim. 6:8).

Let your conversation be without covetousness; and be content with such things as ye have; for he hath said, I will never leave thee, nor forsake thee (Heb. 13:5).

81. What is forbidden in the Tenth Commandment?

A. The Tenth Commandment forbiddeth all *discontentment* with our own estate, *envying or grieving* at the good of our neighbour, and all *inordinate* motions and affections to any thing that is his.

Proofs

Let us not be desirous of vain-glory, provoking one another, envying one another (Gal. 5:26).

And he said unto them, Take heed, and beware of covetousness; for a man's life consisteth not in the abundance of the things which he possesseth (Luke 12:15).

Comment

This commandment refers to the *desires* of our heart. It tells us that we ought not to *covet* — that is, to cherish an unlawful desire for anything belonging to another. And it is put here to warn us that the Law of God is *spiritual*, and is broken by a wrong thought as well as by a wrong act. It commands us to be content with our position in life, whatever that may be. And it forbids us to be fretful over our own want

of success or envious at the good success of others.
To cherish a spirit of *good-will* is the best safeguard
of this command.

12. PENALTY OF THE LAW

82. **Is any man able perfectly to keep the
commandments of God?**

A.   No *mere* man since the Fall is able, in *this* life,
perfectly to keep the commandments of
God, but doth *daily* break them in thought,
word, and deed.

Comment

The Law of God being thus laid before us briefly
in the Ten Commandments, the question arises –
Is any person able to keep this Law. This answer
declares to us that there is none. It says that every
person breaks the Law daily in thought, word, and
act. The only exceptions to this general rule are –
Jesus Christ, Adam before the Fall, and the saints
now in heaven.

Proofs

For there is not a just man upon earth that doeth
good, and sinneth not (Eccles. 7:20).

They are all gone aside, they are all together become filthy; there is none that doeth good, no, not one (Ps. 14:3).

83. Are all transgressions of the law equally heinous?

A.   Some sins, *in themselves*, and by reason of several *aggravations*, are **more heinous** in the sight of God than others.

Comment

This answer tells us that some sins are worse than others. It says that some sins are worse by reason of their own nature, as it is worse to sin against God than against man; and some are worse by reason of certain circumstances, as it is worse to sin deliberately than when hurried by passion.

Proof

And that servant, which knew his lord's will, and prepared not himself, neither did according to his will, shall be beaten with many stripes. But he that knew not, and did commit things worthy of stripes, shall be beaten with few stripes (Luke 12:47, 48).

84. What doth every sin deserve?

A.   Every sin deserveth God's **wrath and curse**, both in *this* life and that which *is to come*.

Comment

The *wrath* of God means his holy displeasure against sin; and his *curse* is the doom which he has pronounced against it. This wrath and this doom, we are told, are the desert of every sin, and stretch over both this life and the life to come.

Proofs

The wages of sin is death (Rom. 6:23).

Then shall he say unto them on the left hand, Depart from me, ye cursed, into everlasting fire, prepared for the devil and his angels (Matt. 25:41).

13. THE WAY TO BE SAVED

85.   What doth God require of us, that we may escape his wrath and curse due to us for sin?

A.   To escape the wrath and curse of God due to us for sin, God requireth of us **faith in Jesus Christ - repentance unto life** – with the diligent use of all the **outward means** whereby Christ communicateth to us the benefits of Redemption.

Comment

The Law of God says, 'Do this and live', or 'Do it not and die'. And man cannot do it. He breaks the Law daily in spite of his utmost efforts. But God is merciful, and has provided a way by which we may be saved. That way is here told us. It consists in faith and repentance, which are *inward* means of salvation, with the diligent use of all the *outward* means hereafter to be told.

Proofs

And saying, The time is fulfilled and the kingdom of God is at hand: repent ye, and believe the gospel (Mark 1:15).

Testifying both to the Jews and also to the Greeks, repentance toward God, and faith toward our Lord Jesus Christ (Acts 20:21).

86. What is Faith in Jesus Christ?

A.   Faith in Jesus Christ is a *saving grace*, whereby we receive and rest upon him

alone for salvation, as he is offered to us in the gospel.

Comment

Grace means undeserved favour or kindness. A saving grace means an act of God's favour ending in salvation. Faith is such a grace. And it is here said to consist in *receiving* Christ – that is, in believing what is said of him in the Bible; and *resting upon him* – that is, trusting our souls to him as our Saviour. We rest on him *alone*, and not in anything we may or can do. Our plea is, *Christ only*.

Proofs

For God so loved the world, that he gave his only begotten Son, that whosoever believeth in him should not perish, but have everlasting life (John 3:16).

Neither is there salvation in any other: for there is none other name under heaven given among men, whereby we must be saved (Acts 4:12).

87. What is Repentance unto Life?

A. Repentance unto Life is a *saving grace*, whereby a sinner – out of a *true sense of his sin*, and apprehension of the *mercy of God in Christ* – doth, with grief and hatred of his sin, **turn from it unto God**, with full purpose of, and endeavour after, *new obedience.*

Comment

Repentance has been called 'the tear of faith'. It springs from a true view of sin, and a clear view of God's mercy in forgiving sin. It consists of two parts: turning from sinful ways with sorrow; and turning to God with an anxious desire to love and serve him. It is called repentance *unto life*, because it leads to eternal life.

Proofs

I tell you, Nay: but, except ye repent, ye shall all likewise perish (Luke 13:3).

And the publican, standing afar off, would not lift up so much as his eyes unto heaven, but smote upon his breast, saying, God be merciful to me a sinner (Luke 18:13).

Wash you, make you clean; put away the evil of your doings from before mine eyes; cease to do evil; learn to do well (Isa. 1:16, 17).

88. What are the outward means whereby Christ communicateth to us the benefits of Redemption?

A.   The outward and ordinary means whereby Christ communicateth to us the benefits of Redemption, are his ordinances; especially the *Word*, *Sacraments*, and *Prayer*; all which are made effectual to the elect for salvation.

Comment

In order that we may be saved, God demands of us not only faith and repentance, but the diligent use of the outward means of grace as well. These outward means are here called *ordinances*, or things which God has *ordained*. They consist mainly in: 1. The study of the Bible; 2. The observance of the Sacraments; 3. The use of Prayer.

Proofs

And they continued steadfastly in the apostles' doctrine and fellowship, and in breaking of bread, and in prayers (Acts 2:42).

And that from a child thou has known the holy scriptures, which are able to make thee wise unto

salvation through faith which is in Christ Jesus
(2 Tim. 3:15).

14. THE BIBLE AS A MEANS OF GRACE

89. How is the Word made effectual to salvation?

A   The Spirit of God maketh the *reading*, but
      especially the *preaching* of the Word, an
      effectual means of *convincing* and *converting*
      sinners, and of *building them up* in holiness
      and comfort, through faith, unto salvation.

Comment

In order that the Bible may make us wise unto
salvation, two things are necessary: the Holy Spirit's
influence on God's part, and a diligent study of it on
ours. When these two things go together, men are
convinced of their sin and brought to Christ. They are
made holier in their lives, and happier in their hearts.

Proofs

The law of the LORD is perfect, converting the
soul: the testimony of the LORD is sure, making
wise the simple (Ps. 19:7).

All scripture is given by inspiration of God and is profitable for doctrine, for reproof, for correction, for instruction in righteousness (2 Tim. 3:16).

90. How is the Word to be read and heard, that it may become effectual to salvation?

A.   That the Word may become effectual to salvation, we must attend thereunto with *diligence*, *preparation*, and *prayer*, receive it with *faith and love*, lay it up in our *hearts*, and practise it in our *lives*.

Comment

We are here taught the proper way to use the Bible. We must use it carefully, reverently, and prayerfully. We must believe what it tells us, and do what it bids us. And we must receive the truth in the love of it, else the Word read will not profit our souls.

Proofs

Open thou mine eyes, that I may behold wondrous things out of thy law (Ps. 119:18).

The word preached did not profit them, not being mixed with faith in them that heard it (Heb. 4:2).

Thy word have I hid in mine heart, that I might not sin against thee (Ps. 119:11).

If any man will do his will, he shall know of the doctrine, whether it be of God, or whether I speak of myself (John 7:17).

15. THE SACRAMENTS AS A MEANS OF GRACE

91. **How do the sacraments become effectual means of salvation?**

A. The sacraments become effectual means of salvation – not from any *virtue* in them, or in him that doth administer them – but only by the **blessing of Christ**, and the **working of his Spirit** in them that by faith receive them.

Comment

We are here taught the proper way of using the sacraments. We must pray for the blessing of Christ on them. It was he who appointed them, and it is he alone who can make them of benefit to our souls. In themselves the sacraments are of no value, nor can the minister (notwithstanding what the Roman Catholic Church says) give them any power whatever apart from Christ.

Proofs

For he that eateth and drinketh unworthily, eateth and drinketh damnation to himself, not discerning the Lord's body (1 Cor. 11:29).

So then neither is he that planteth any thing, neither he that watereth; but God that giveth the increase (1 Cor. 3:7).

92. What is a sacrament?

A.   A sacrament is an holy *ordinance* instituted by Christ, wherein, – *by sensible signs* – Christ, and the benefits of the New Covenant, are represented, sealed, and applied to believers.

Comment

We are here taught that the marks of a sacrament are: 1. That it is appointed by Christ; 2. That it is a way of teaching the gospel by *outward signs*. Its uses are three in number: 1. To *represent* the gospel to us, or teach it plainly; 2. To *seal* the gospel to us, or confirm our faith in it; 3. To *apply* the gospel to us, or bring it home to our hearts. The word *sacrament* is derived from a Latin word, which signified the sacred oath of fidelity to his commander, which the soldier took on entering the army for the service of his country. In a Christian sense, it means the vow of fidelity and obedience to Christ which is taken when we enter the Church. This vow was taken for us in Baptism, when we were infants. In the Lord's Supper, we take it upon ourselves.

Proofs

This is my covenant, which ye shall keep, between me and you and thy seed after thee; Every man-child among you shall be circumcised (Gen. 17:10).

And he received the sign of circumcision, a seal of the righteousness of the faith which he had yet being uncircumcised: that he might be the father of all them that believe, though they be not circumcised; that righteousness might be imputed unto them also (Rom. 4:11).

93. Which are the sacraments of the New Testament?

A.   The sacraments of the New Testament are, *Baptism*, and the *Lord's Supper*.

Comment

The two sacraments of the Old Testament were Circumcision and the Passover. The two sacraments of the New Testament are Baptism and the Lord's Supper. These sacraments answer the one to the other – Baptism coming in place of Circumcision, and the Lord's Supper in place of the Passover. They teach likewise the same truths – Circumcision and Baptism teaching the necessity of being *born again*, and the Passover and the Lord's Supper teaching the necessity of a *sacrifice for sin*.

Proofs

Go ye therefore, and teach all nations, baptizing them in the name of the Father, and of the Son, and of the Holy Ghost (Matt. 28:19).

And as they were eating, Jesus took bread, and blessed it, and brake it, and gave it to the disciples, and said, Take, eat; this is my body (Matt. 26:26).

16. BAPTISM

94. What is Baptism?

A. Baptism is a sacrament, wherein the *washing with water* – in the name of the Father, and of the Son, and of the Holy Ghost – doth signify and seal our *ingrafting into Christ*, and *partaking of the benefits* of the Covenant of Grace, and our *engagement* to be the Lord's.

Comment

The *outward act* in baptism is washing with water in the name of the Father, and of the Son, and of the Holy Ghost. The *inward meaning* of this is the removal of our sin. We are all by nature born in sin, and we need to be *born again* before we can be admitted into heaven. Now, Baptism is an emblem of this new birth. And the baptismal fountain of water tells of *another fountain*, which is filled with the blood of Jesus Christ, and which has been opened freely for all sins and uncleanness.

Proofs

Go ye therefore, and teach all nations, baptizing them in the name of the Father, and of the Son, and of the Holy Ghost (Matt. 28:19).

Know ye not, that so many of us as were baptized into Jesus Christ were baptized into his death? (Rom. 6:3).

95. To whom is Baptism to be administered?

A.   Baptism is *not* to be administered to any that are out of the visible Church – *till they profess their faith in Christ*, and *obedience* to him; but the *infants of such as are members* of the visible church are to be baptized.

Comment

We are here taught the persons who may be baptized. They consist of two classes – *adults* who are Christians, but who may not have been already baptized; and the *infants* of church members. The former are baptized because the meaning of the ordinance is to declare that the persons baptized profess themselves to be Christians; and the latter are baptized because the promises of God to his people extend to their children as well as to themselves.

Proofs

Then they that gladly received his word were baptized, and the same day there were added unto them about three thousand souls (Acts 2:41).

For the promise is unto you, and to your children,
and to all that are afar off, even as many as the Lord
our God shall call (Acts 2:39).

17. THE LORD'S SUPPER

96. What is the Lord's Supper?

A.   The Lord's Supper is a sacrament, wherein
by giving and *receiving bread and wine,
according to Christ's appointment*, his **death**
is showed forth; and the worthy receivers
are – not after a corporal and carnal manner
– but *by faith* made partakers of his *body and
blood*, with all his benefits, to their spiritual
nourishment and growth in grace.

Comment

The Lord's Supper is so called because it is a feast
instituted by our *Lord Jesus Christ*. It is likewise called
the *Communion*. The *outward act* in it is eating bread and
drinking wine, according to Christ's appointment;
and the *inward meaning* of it is the sacrifice of Christ
– the broken bread telling of his broken body, and
the poured-out wine telling of his shed blood. In
itself it is of no value whatsoever, but when received

in faith it quickens our love to God, deepens our faith in Christ, and promotes the welfare of our souls. The Roman Catholic Church teaches that the bread in the Communion is changed into the *actual flesh* of our Lord; but this is an error. We can only receive Christ by faith.

Proofs

For I have received of the Lord that which also I delivered unto you, That the Lord Jesus the same night in which he was betrayed took bread, etc. (1 Cor. 11:23).

The cup of blessing which we bless, is it not the communion of the blood of Christ? The bread which we break, is it not the communion of the body of Christ? (1 Cor. 10:16).

97.   What is required to the worthy receiving of the Lord's Supper?

A.   It is required of them that would worthily partake of the Lord's Supper, that they examine themselves of their *knowledge to discern the Lord's body*, of their *faith to feed upon him*, of their *repentance, love, and new obedience*;

lest, coming unworthily, they eat and drink judgment to themselves.

Comment

We are here taught the proper qualifications for receiving the Lord's Supper. They are: 1. *Knowledge* sufficient to understand what is represented by it; 2. *Faith* sufficient to believe that as the bread which we eat sustains our bodies, so the Bread of Life which it represents will sustain our souls; 3. *Repentance* from all known sin; 4. *Love* to God and man; 5. A resolution henceforth to act up to every known *duty*.

Proofs

But let a man examine himself, and so let him eat of that bread and drink of that cup. For he that eateth and drinketh unworthily, eateth and drinketh damnation to himself, not discerning the Lord's body (1 Cor. 11:28, 29).

Examine yourselves, whether ye be in the faith (2 Cor. 13:5).

Let us keep the feast, not with old leaven, neither with the leaven of malice and wickedness; but with the unleavened bread of sincerity and truth (1 Cor. 5:8).

18. PRAYER AS A MEANS OF GRACE

98. What is prayer?

A. Prayer is an offering up of our desires unto God, for things *agreeable to his will*, in the name of **Christ**, with confession of *our sins*, and thankful acknowledgment of *his mercies*.

Comment

Prayer means *asking* of God; and we are here told the following three things respecting it: 1. As to its *form*, it should be offered to God in the name of Christ; 2. As to its *substance*, it should be for things agreeable to God's will; 3. As to its *manner*, it should be made with humble acknowledgement of our sins, and grateful acknowledgement of God's mercy.

Proofs

Ask, and it shall be given you; seek, and ye shall find; knock, and it shall be opened unto you (Matt. 7:7).

Verily, verily, I say unto you, Whatsoever ye shall ask the Father in my name, he will give it you (John 16:23).

Be careful for nothing; but in every thing by prayer and supplication with thanksgiving let your requests be made known unto God (Phil. 4:6).

99. What rule hath God given for our direction in prayer?

A. The *whole Word of God* is of use to direct us in prayer; but the *special* rule of direction is that form of prayer which Christ taught his disciples, commonly called **the Lord's Prayer**.

Comment

We are here taught that in praying to God we have the whole Bible as a guide. But specially we have a pattern or example set us in the prayer which Christ taught his disciples. This is usually called the Lord's Prayer – that is, the prayer of the Lord Jesus Christ.

Proofs

And this is the confidence that we have in him, that, if we ask any thing according to his will, he heareth us (1 John 5:14).

After this manner therefore pray ye: Our Father which art in heaven, Hallowed be thy name, etc. (Matt. 6:9).

19. THE LORD'S PRAYER

100. What doth the Preface of the Lord's Prayer teach us?

A.   The preface of the Lord's Prayer – (which is, **Our Father which art in Heaven**) – teacheth us to draw near to God with all holy *reverence* and *confidence* – as children to a father, able and ready to help us; – and that we should pray *with* and *for* others.

Comment

Preface means *introduction* or *beginning*. And we here learn that the Preface of the Lord's Prayer teaches us three things: 1. That we should draw near to God *reverently*, seeing he is in *heaven*; 2. That we should draw near *confidently*, seeing he is our *Father*; 3. That we should pray along with others, and for them, seeing he is *our* Father.

Proofs

After this manner therefore pray ye: Our Father which art in heaven, Hallowed be thy name (Matt. 6:9).

For ye have not received the spirit of bondage again to fear; but ye have received the Spirit of adoption, whereby we cry, Abba, Father (Rom. 8:15).

Be not wroth very sore, O LORD, neither remember iniquity for ever: behold, see, we beseech thee, we are all thy people (Isa. 64:9).

101. What do we pray for in the First Petition?

A.   In the First Petition – (which is, **hallowed be thy name**) – we pray, That God would enable us and others to *glorify* him in all that whereby he maketh himself known; – and that he would dispose all things to his own glory.

Comment

A petition means *something asked*. In the Lord's Prayer there are six petitions – the first three being about God, and the last three about ourselves. In the first of these petitions we ask two things: that God's name be hallowed or glorified by all *men*, and that it be hallowed or glorified by all *events*.

Proofs

Let the people praise thee, O God; let all the people praise thee (Ps. 67:3).

For of him, and through him, and to him, are all things: to whom be glory for ever. Amen (Rom. 11:36).

102. What do we pray for in the Second Petition?

A.   In the Second Petition – (which is, **Thy Kingdom come**) – we pray, That *Satan's kingdom* may be destroyed; and that the *kingdom of Grace* may be advanced, ourselves and others brought into it, and kept in it; and that the *kingdom of Glory* may be hastened.

Comment

A kingdom means a people who are ruled by a king. Now, there are three kingdoms mentioned here: the *kingdom of Satan*, or those who obey Satan; the *kingdom of Grace*, or those who obey God; and the *kingdom of Glory*, or those who will reign with Christ in glory. In this petition we ask that the first of these be destroyed, that the second may prosper, and that the time of the third may speedily arrive.

Proofs

Let God arise, let his enemies be scattered: let them also that hate him flee before him (Ps. 68:1).

Do good in thy good pleasure unto Zion: build thou the walls of Jerusalem (Ps. 51:18).

He which testifieth these things saith, Surely I come quickly. Amen. Even so, come, Lord Jesus (Rev. 22:20).

103. What do we pray for in the Third Petition?

A.   In the Third Petition – (which is, **Thy will be done in Earth, as it is in Heaven**) – we pray, That God, by his grace, would make us able and willing to *know*, *obey*, and *submit to his will* in all things, as the angels do in heaven.

Comment

God's *will* means what he wishes to be done. This will is obeyed perfectly in heaven, and in this petition we pray that it may be obeyed as perfectly on earth. This can never be done in our own strength, and therefore we ask that God would help us to know perfectly what his will is, and having learned it, to do and suffer it.

Proofs

Give me understanding, and I shall keep thy law; yea, I shall observe it with my whole heart (Ps. 119:34).

And he went a little farther, and fell on his face, and prayed, saying, O my Father, if it be possible, let this cup pass from me: nevertheless not as I will, but as thou wilt (Matt. 26:39).

104. What do we pray for in the Fourth Petition?

A.   In the Fourth Petition – (which is, **Give us this day our daily bread**) – we pray, That of God's free gift we may receive a *competent portion* of the good things of this life, and enjoy *his blessing* with them.

Comment

We now come to the petitions concerning ourselves – the *order* of the prayer being God *first*, and *ourselves afterwards*. In this petition we pray for the supply of our bodily wants. We ask for two things – a sufficient portion for the day, and God's blessing with it.

Proofs

Remove far from me vanity and lies: give me neither poverty nor riches; feed me with food convenient for me (Prov. 30:8).

And let the beauty of the LORD our God be upon us: and establish thou the work of our hands upon us; yea, the work of our hands establish thou it (Ps. 90:17).

105. What do we pray for in the Fifth Petition?

A. In the Fifth Petition – (which is, **and forgive us our debts, as we forgive our debtors**) – we pray, That God, for Christ's sake, would freely *pardon all our sins*; which we are the rather encouraged to ask, because by his grace we are enabled from the heart to *forgive others*.

Comment

In the Fifth and Sixth Petitions we pray for the supply of our spiritual wants. We ask first for the pardon of our sins. This is promised in Scripture on the condition that we forgive others. If God, then, has enabled us to forgive all who have offended us, we may confidently trust that he will hear our own prayer for forgiveness. Sins are here called *debts*, because in sinning we become debtors to the law; and the law demands either obedience, or the penalty of disobedience.

Proofs

Have mercy upon me, O God, according to thy loving-kindness; according unto the multitude of thy tender mercies blot out my transgressions (Ps. 51:1).

For if ye forgive men their trespasses, your heavenly Father will also forgive you (Matt. 6:14).

106. What do we pray for in the Sixth Petition?

A.   In the Sixth Petition – (which is, and lead us not into temptation, but deliver us from evil) – we pray, That God would *either keep us* from being tempted to sin, or *support and deliver us* when we *are* tempted.

Comment

Temptation means anything that would induce us to sin. And in this petition we ask one of two things from God – either that he would take all temptation away from us, or that he would enable us to resist and overcome it.

Proofs

Watch and pray, that ye enter not into temptation: the spirit indeed is willing, but the flesh is weak (Matt. 26:41).

Keep back thy servant also from presumptuous sins; let them not have dominion over me (Ps. 19:13).

And the Lord shall deliver me from every evil work, and will preserve me unto his heavenly kingdom: to whom be glory for ever and ever. Amen (2 Tim. 4:18).

107. What doth the conclusion of the Lord's Prayer teach us?

A. The conclusion of the Lord's Prayer – (which is, **For thine is the Kingdom. and the Power, and the Glory, For ever, Amen**) – teacheth us to take our encouragement in prayer from **God** only, and in our prayers to *praise* him, ascribing kingdom, power and glory to him. – And, in testimony of our *desire*, and *assurance* to be heard, we say, **Amen**.

Comment

The conclusion means the *end*. And the concluding part of the Lord's Prayer teaches us three things: 1. that we should look to God alone for help; 2. that we should give all praise to him who alone can answer our prayers; 3. and that we should end all our prayers with some such word as Amen, which means, *May it be so*, or *May our prayers be heard*.

Proofs

O thou that hearest prayer, unto thee shall all flesh come (Ps. 65:2).

Thine, O Lord, is the greatness, and the power, and the glory, and the victory, and the majesty: for all that is in the heaven and in the earth is thine; thine is the kingdom, O Lord, and thou art exalted as head above all (1 Chron. 29:11).

Let all the people say, Amen (Ps. 106:48).

REVISING QUESTIONS

(1)Who made us? For what purpose did he make us? How may we glorify God? Where will we enjoy him for ever? Why is the glorifying of God put before the enjoying of him? For what purpose do most men seem to think they were made?

(2) Could we know of ourselves what God wishes us to do? Where do we learn his will? What are the two divisions of the Bible? Why is it so divided? What Church holds the Bible *not* to be the only rule of faith and manners? Prove this to be an error.

(3) What does the Bible tell us regarding God? What regarding man? Why does the Bible tell us what to believe as well as what to do?

(4) Can anyone see God? Why? What kind of a Spirit is he? What is his character?

(5) How many Gods are there? How is he distinguished from all other objects of worship? Who believe in many Gods?

(6) How many persons are in the Godhead? Which of them is greatest? Are not these three persons three

gods? Can we understand this? Why, then, do we believe it? Who will not believe in a Trinity?

(7) Who is the Ruler of the world? What do you mean by his *decrees*? When did he fore-appoint all things? Will everything that he appoints come to pass? What end had he in view when he decreed all things?

(8) In how many ways does God work out his purposes? What is the distinction between the two? Does he still execute his decrees in both these ways?

(9) Who created all things? What is the difference between *creating* and *making*? By what means did God create all things? In what *time*? In what *condition*? Do they still remain very good?

(10) Who created man? On what day of creation was he made? Was it his body or his soul that was made in God's image? In what did the first man resemble God? Do we resemble God in these endowments now?

(11) What does the word *providence* mean? Who keeps all things in life? Could they not live of themselves? Who overrules all our action? In what manner? Can we not then do as we choose? (Prov. 16:9; Ps. 76:10)

(12) What is a covenant? What was the covenant of life? Between whom was it made? What was the first command God gave to Adam? What was to be the punishment of disobedience? What was to be the reward of obedience?

(13) Who were our first parents? Did they keep their covenant with God? What change then occurred in their state? What change occurred in the place of their abode?

(14) What are the two kinds of sins? Give instances of each kind. What is the law of God? Where is it contained?

(15) What was the first sin? Give an account of it.

(16) What was the covenant of life? Did Adam *alone* suffer the consequences of his sin? Who suffered with him? Why? Who was exempt from all connexion with Adam's guilt? Why?

(17) What is the Fall? What have been the consequences of it to us?

(18) What is the distinction between original and actual sin? What does original sin include? How may all actual sins be traced up to the Fall? Are we blameable for original sin?

(19) Name the particulars of the state of misery due to the Fall. Explain each. Is this the condition in which we are all born?

(20) What is the covenant of grace? Another name for it? With whom was it made? For what purpose was it made? Why is it called the covenant of grace? Distinguish between it and the covenant of life. What moved God to appoint some to everlasting life? What would have become *of us all* if he had not done so?

(21) What is it to redeem? Who is our Redeemer? From what does he redeem us? What price did he pay for our ransom? What natures has he? Was he always man? Is he God and man *now*?

(22) Of how many parts does our nature consist? What had Christ beside these? How did Christ become man and not inherit original sin? Why had Christ to become man? (Job 9:33)

(23) What is the distinction between the last section and this? What three offices are discharged by Christ as our Redeemer? To what end did he undertake this threefold service? When did he do so?

(24) What is a prophet? Name several. What is that which Christ as a prophet more especially reveals

to us? What means does he employ in doing so? Wherein does Christ excel or surpass all other prophets? (1 Pet. 1:10, 11)

(25) What is a priest? Name several. Are there any priests now? Why not? What sacrifice did Christ offer? For what purpose did he die? Wherein does Christ excel all other priests? (Heb. 10:1)

(26) What is a king? What are his duties? What do you mean by his *subduing* us to himself? Who are the enemies Christ defends us from? Wherein does Christ differ from all other kings? (John 18:36,37)

(27) What is the meaning of *humiliation*? Mention the eight particulars in which Christ's humiliation consisted.

(28) What is the meaning of *exaltation*? Mention the four particulars in which Christ's exaltation consists. Why is it said that his humiliation *consisted*, and his exaltation *consisteth*?

(29) Who appointed the plan of salvation? Who accomplished it? Who makes that salvation ours?

(30) By what act on our part are we saved? What is faith? Who implants it in us? How does faith save us?

(31) By how many different ways does God call us to believe on his Son? Which of these is effectual? Are we then innocent, though we give no heed to the outward call? Name the four different steps by which the Spirit leads us to salvation. If a man receive effectual calling, is he certainly saved?

(32) When are the blessings of salvation enjoyed? Are they all given at once? Mention the order in which they are bestowed.

(33) What does Justification mean? Why is it called an act? Why of God's free grace? What are the two parts of it? What is the distinction between the two? How can God righteously justify the unjust? How does Christ's righteousness become ours?

(34) What does Adoption mean? What are the two parts of it? Who are members of God's family? Of what family are the wicked?

(35) What does Sanctification mean? Why is it called a work? Why is it called a *renewing*? Who performs it in us? Can we not do it ourselves? What does it consist in? Explain this. Show how Justification, Adoption, and Sanctification are all necessary to our full salvation.

(36) What are the five minor blessings which flow from the three principal ones? Explain each of them.

(37) Repeat the blessings which God bestows upon his people in this life. At what other periods do they receive still further benefits? What are the respective blessings of the soul and the body at death?

(38) What follows death? What follows the resurrection? With what bodies shall believers appear at the judgment? What shall Christ say to his people on that day? Where shall his people then dwell? Where do the souls of believers dwell in the interval betwixt death and the resurrection?

(39) What is duty? Whose will ought we to obey? What kind of obedience does God require?

(40, 41) What is the Moral Law? Where was it placed at first? Where afterwards? Why had God to place it in the Scriptures? Where is it briefly stated? Where fully stated?

(42) What two commandments may the ten be reduced to? In what manner are we to love God? In what manner are we to love our neighbour? What parable teaches this latter duty?

(43, 44) What is a preface? What is the preface to the Ten Commandments? Why did God make a preface to them? State the three arguments he uses. How does this preface still apply to us?

(45-48) Who wrote the Ten Commandments? On what were they written? What did the first table contain? What the second? How does the *Shorter Catechism* explain each commandment? Repeat the First Commandment. State the four things it bids us do. State the three things it forbids us to do. What is the special reason given for observing this commandment?

(49-52) Repeat the Second Commandment. How does it differ from the first? What kind of sins does it warn us against? Has God told us the way in which he wishes to be worshipped? Where? What are some of the usual ordinances of worship? What are the four things this commandment bids us to do? What are the two things it forbids us to do? State the three special reasons given for its observance. What does *propriety* mean here? Show from the conclusion of this commandment that God delighteth in mercy.

(53-56) Repeat the Third Commandment. How does it differ from the second? What kind of sins does it warn us against? By what five things does

God make himself known? How must we treat these? How must we beware of treating them? How do men treat the breakers of this commandment? How will God treat them? Mention one instance in which a breach of this commandment is punished by law – Perjury. Is an oath under all circumstances forbidden? (Matt. 26:63)

(57-62) Repeat the Fourth Commandment. Why is the word *remember* here used? What duty does it require of us? State in few words what the first four commandments enjoin. When was the Sabbath first appointed? On what day of the week? What was it intended to commemorate? On what day is it now kept? What is it intended to remind us of? When was the change made? What authority have we for making the change? What does the word *Sabbath* mean? Of what is it an emblem? From what kind of work should we rest? What exceptions are made? What are works of necessity? What are works of mercy? Why are these exceptions made? (Mark 2:27). How should we employ our time on the Sabbath? Repeat the four special reasons for keeping this commandment. Give the parts of the commandment itself in which these are mentioned.

(63-66) Repeat the Fifth Commandment. What kind of duties does it command? What kind of sins does it forbid? In what table of the law does it stand? What does the second table treat of? What do you mean by *honouring* your parents? Are we to do this although we may not think them worthy? Are we to obey them in doing wrong? Why not? (Eph. 6:1). What promise has God made to those who keep this commandment? To whom was this promise first made? What did it mean to them?

(67-69) Repeat the Sixth Commandment. What kind of duties does it enjoin? What kind of sins does it forbid? How does it include the taking care of our health? What two crimes are here forbidden? Is it always wrong to take away another's life? Mention cases in which it may be allowable. How did our Saviour include *anger* as breach of this command?

(70-72) Repeat the Seventh Commandment. What kind of duties does it enjoin? What kind of sins does it forbid? In how many ways are we to preserve chastity?

(73-75) Repeat the Eighth Commandment. What two things does it require? What two things does it forbid? Is it wrong to become rich? Is it right to allow ourselves to become poor if we can help it? In what way only may we strive to acquire wealth? What is the difference between wealth and outward estate? What virtue, beside honesty, is commended to us here? (1 Tim. 5:8)

(76-78) Repeat the Ninth Commandment. What is meant by bearing false witness? What two things does this commandment require? What is the difference between *maintaining* and *promoting* truth? What two things does it forbid? What are the common names of these sins? What is meant by the *good name* of any one?

(79-81) Repeat the Tenth Commandment. What is meant by coveting? Wherein does this commandment differ from all the others? What two things does it require? What three things does it forbid? What great lesson did Paul learn from this commandment? (Rom. 7:7) What is the best safeguard against breaking it?

(82-84) Does any man live a day without sin? Has any man ever done so? Show, in the words of the answer, how the following persons are excepted: Jesus Christ, Adam in Paradise, the saints in heaven. Whether are transgressions of the first or the second table of the law the worse? Which is the most heinous sin under the second table? (Num. 35:31). What is the most heinous of all sins? (Matt. 12:31). What does the least heinous sin deserve? What is the difference between

God's wrath and God's curse? How long will these last against sinners?

(85-88) Does the Law show any way of escape from its penalty? What does? What are the inward means the Gospel requires us to use? What are the outward means? What are the two parts of faith? What is the difference between receiving and resting upon Christ? For what purpose do we rest upon Christ? What else might we be tempted to rest on? (Rom. 3:28). What has Repentance been called? What two steps does it include? Why are both necessary? With what feelings do we turn from sin? With what disposition do we turn to God? Mention the three *ordinances* here stated. Why are they called ordinances? What is the object of them?

(89, 90) What is the use of the Bible? What two things are necessary that it may benefit us? When these are both given, what four results follow? What is the proper way to use the Bible? Why should our way of using the Bible differ from our way of using any other book? If we do not practise the Bible, will we ever fully know it? (John 7:17).

(91-93) What is the second of the outward means of grace? Name them. What is the right way of using them? What is the wrong way? May we expect the blessing of Christ in the use of his own ordinances?

What are the distinguishing marks of a sacrament? What are the benefits we may derive from it? What are the two Old Testament sacraments? What are the two New Testament ones? How does the one answer to the other? What is the original meaning of the word *sacrament*? What is its *Christian meaning*?

(94, 95) What is the element used in baptism? What does it stand for? What is done with the water? What does that represent? What is the difference between baptism *signifying* the truths of the gospel and *sealing* them? What two classes of persons may be admitted to baptism? Why the former? Why the latter? Was not the rite of circumcision allowed in similar cases?

(96, 97) Why is the Lord's Supper so called? Another name for it? What are the elements used in it? What do they signify? What is the outward act in the Lord's Supper? What does that represent? In what manner do we live upon Christ? What error does this guard us against? Mention five things requisite to the proper partaking of the Lord's Supper. If we have not these, will we receive any good from this sacrament? Will we receive any evil? Why should we partake of the Lord's Supper? When should we do so? What are the proper qualifications for receiving it?

(98, 99) What does the word *prayer* mean? What do we ask God for? Why do we pray in the name of Christ? With what dispositions ought we pray? How do we know that God hears our prayers? What is the general guide for teaching us to pray? What is the particular pattern? Why is it called *the Lord's* Prayer?

(100-107) How many petitions are in the Lord's Prayer? Whom do the first three petitions concern? Whom the last three? What is a preface? What three lessons does this preface teach us? Point out the words from which we draw these lessons. In how many ways should God's name be hallowed? What are the three things included in the second petition? What do you mean by God's will? Where has he revealed it? Do we obey that will perfectly? Who do so? What is the fourth petition concerning? How much do we ask for? And what along with it? What does the fifth petition ask for? What argument do we use here? If we forgive not others, will we ourselves be forgiven? Why are sins called *debts*? In what form are we taught to put the sixth petition? Why in this form? Why do we believe that God is willing to hear our prayers? (see Preface) Why do we believe that he is *able* to answer them? (See conclusion). What is the meaning of *Amen*?

Christian Focus Publications

Our mission statement –

STAYING FAITHFUL
In dependence upon God we seek to impact the world through literature faithful to His infallible Word, the Bible. Our aim is to ensure that the Lord Jesus Christ is presented as the only hope to obtain forgiveness of sin, live a useful life and look forward to heaven with Him.

Our books are published in four imprints:

CHRISTIAN FOCUS

Popular works including biographies, commentaries, basic doctrine and Christian living.

CHRISTIAN HERITAGE

Books representing some of the best material from the rich heritage of the church.

MENTOR

Books written at a level suitable for Bible College and seminary students, pastors, and other serious readers. The imprint includes commentaries, doctrinal studies, examination of current issues and church history.

CF4•K

Children's books for quality Bible teaching and for all age groups: Sunday school curriculum, puzzle and activity books; personal and family devotional titles, biographies and inspirational stories – Because you are never too young to know Jesus!

Christian Focus Publications Ltd,
Geanies House, Fearn, Ross-shire,
IV20 1TW, Scotland, United Kingdom.
www.christianfocus.com